Understanding Integrated Reporting

The Concise Guide to Integrated Thinking and the Future of Corporate Reporting

T0298877

Carol A. Adams

Director, Integrated Horizons

Tw: @ProfCarolAdams

e: carol.adams@integrated-horizons.com

Integrated Horizons: http://integrated-horizons.com

Towards Sustainable Business: http://drcaroladams.net

First published in 2013 by Dō Sustainability (Updated 2015)
87 Lonsdale Road, Oxford OX2 7ET, UK

ISBN 978-1-909293-85-4 (eBook-ePub)
ISBN 978-1-909293-86-1 (eBook-PDF)
ISBN 978-1-909293-84-7 (Paperback)

A catalogue record for this title is available from the British Library.

Dō Sustainability strives for net positive social and environmental impact. See our sustainability policy at **www.dosustainability.com**.

Page design and typesetting by Alison Rayner
Cover by Becky Chilcott

For further information on Dō Sustainability, visit our website:
www.dosustainability.com

DōShorts

Dō Sustainability is the publisher of DōShorts: short, high-value ebooks that distil sustainability best practice and business insights for busy, results-driven professionals. Each DōShort can be read in 90 minutes.

New and forthcoming DōShorts – stay up to date

We publish 3 to 5 new DōShorts each month. The best way to keep up to date? Sign up to our short, monthly newsletter. Go to **www.dosustainability.com/newsletter** to sign up to the Dō Newsletter. Some of our latest and forthcoming titles include:

- *Adapting to Climate Change: 2.0 Enterprise Risk Management*
  Mark Trexler & Laura Kosloff

- *How to Engage Youth to Drive Corporate Responsbility: Roles and Interventions*   Nicolò Wojewoda

- *The Short Guide to Sustainable Investing*   Cary Krosinsky

- *Strategic Sustainability: Why it Matters to Your Business and How to Make it Happen*   Alexandra McKay

- *Sustainability Decoded: How to Unlock Profit Through the Value Chain*   Laura Musikanski

- *Working Collaboratively: A Practical Guide to Achieving More*
  Penny Walker

- *Understanding G4: The Concise Guide to Next Generation Sustainability Reporting*   Elaine Cohen

- *Leading Sustainable Innovation*   Nick Coad & Paul Pritchard

- *Leadership for Sustainability and Change*   Cynthia Scott & Tammy Esteves

- *The Social Licence to Operate: Your Management Framework for Complex Times* Leeora Black
- *Building a Sustainable Supply Chain* Gareth Kane
- *Management Systems for Sustainability: How to Successfully Connect Strategy and Action* Phil Cumming

Subscriptions

In addition to individual sales of our ebooks, we now offer subscriptions. Access 60+ ebooks for the price of 5 with a personal subscription to our full e-library. Institutional subscriptions are also available for your staff or students. Visit **www.dosustainability.com/books/subscriptions** or email **veruschka@dosustainability.com**

Write for us, or suggest a DōShort

Please visit **www.dosustainability.com** for our full publishing programme. If you don't find what you need, write for us! Or suggest a DōShort on our website. We look forward to hearing from you.

Abstract

INTEGRATED REPORTING <IR> is the big new development in corporate reporting that everyone is talking about. This DōShort is a practical guide explaining in simple terms what it is, how to do it and why you should. <IR> (IIRC, 2013a) is not just for companies – elements of <IR> are relevant to any organisation. Integrated reporting is a paradigm shift pushing the boundaries around how organisations think about their business model and how they create value. This Short demonstrates how integrated thinking and <IR> can benefit many other organisations whose success and influence depends on relationships and partnerships. The Short will answer your questions about how to approach integrated thinking and <IR> and identify examples to follow.

About the Author

CAROL ADAMS is a Director of Integrated Horizons (**www.integrated-horizons.com**) providing advice to senior executives and finance professionals in companies, public sector organisations and NGOs. She writes on topical issues at Towards Sustainable Business (**www.drcaroladams.net**). Carol has held senior management positions including leading the development of award-winning management and governance processes and sustainability reports; the first winning two best first-time report awards and the second ranked fifth in international awards (**www. corporateregister.com**).

She is a member of the Stakeholder Council of the Global Reporting Initiative and was a member of the Capitals Technical Collaboration Group which developed the IIRC's Capitals Background Paper (IIRC, 2013b; **www.theiirc.org/resources-2/framework-development/background-papers/**). She is a member of the ICAS Sustainability Committee and the ACCA's Global Forum on Sustainability. Carol qualified as a member of the Institute of Chartered Accountants of Scotland, holds an MSc in Accounting and Finance (LSE) and a PhD in international corporate reporting (University of Glasgow). An internationally renowned author in sustainability reporting, change management and performance management (including *Accountability, Social Responsibility and Sustainability*, Pearson ISBN: 9780273681380, other publications[1] and pieces in the media[2]), Carol holds a part-time research professor position at Monash University, a visiting professorship at the Adam Smith Business School, University of Glasgow and an Honorary Research Fellowship at Centre for Sustainability Management, Leuphana Universität Lüneburg.

....

Disclaimer

THIS BOOK IS NOT AN OFFICIAL PUBLICATION of the International Integrated Reporting Council (IIRC). It has been reviewed by the IIRC with respect to accuracy of quotations from the International Integrated Reporting '<IR>' Framework (IIRC, 2013a). All opinions expressed are those of the author. This work of the author is based on her understanding and interpretation of the International <IR> Framework and supporting material and other integrated reporting initiatives as current at the date of publication.

Every effort has been made by the author to present integrated reporting initiatives in a balanced and accurate manner. The author does not accept liability for errors or interpretations not intended by integrated reporting frameworks or guidelines, organisations that publish integrated reports, or for future changes to frameworks which may affect the guidance provided in this book.

Note

<IR> can be adopted by a wide range of organisations including companies, public sector organisations, universities, not-for-profit organisations and NGOs. The term 'corporate reporting' in this book is used to refer to the reporting by any type of organisation to providers of capital/funds and other stakeholders.

Acknowledgments

THE AUTHOR IS GRATEFUL for the cooperation of Paul Druckman and the IIRC in providing materials to assist with the timely release of this book and to Ian Jameson from the IIRC, Nick Bellorini from DōSustainability and anonymous reviewers for providing valuable feedback on the book proposal and drafts of the text. Thanks are also due to those who provided quotes for inclusion in the book.

Acronyms

<IR>	Integrated Reporting
CSR	Corporate Social Responsibility
ESG	Environment, Social and Governance
GRI	Global Reporting Initiative
IIRC	International Integrated Reporting Council
IFRS	International Financial Reporting Standards
NFP	Not-for-profit
CEO	Chief Executive Officer
CFO	Chief Financial Officer
CSO	Chief Sustainability Officer

A glossary of terms used in the context of <IR> is provided in the International <IR> Framework. See the index to this book for discussion of key terms.

Why I Wrote This Book

I AM AN ACCOUNTANT who has specialised in international financial reporting, sustainability reporting, other aspects of non-financial reporting and governance. I take the view, informed by research, leadership and advisory work, that corporate accountability for social and environmental impacts is poor. Sometimes there is a deliberate attempt to hide or deceive and sometimes there is a reluctance to disclose the activities the organisation is involved in which add value to society.

I wrote this book because I believe <IR> is the best hope I've seen for a while of improving the relationship between business, society and the environment. <IR> provides the possibility at least of a transformational change by encouraging organisations to act in their own best interests adding value to society and protecting the natural environment. And for those that are simply shy about disclosing good work, it gives them a reason to do so and to see Corporate Social Responsibility (CSR) and sustainability as a necessary part of creating value to the organisation.

Corporate greed will continue as will the shortcuts and lack of accountability that fuel it. <IR> will not remove the need for regulatory pressure and stakeholder action, but it can play a part. <IR> gives companies an opportunity to demonstrate innovation.

The work I have done aimed at contributing to the embedding of citizenship and sustainability through research, advisory work, senior management, report preparation, guideline and standard setting has highlighted to me that the most important determinant of success is CEO, CFO and Board support. <IR> has the potential to increase understanding of the importance of (and therefore support for) incorporating social and environmental issues into long-term decision-making and the impact of doing so on an organisation's ability to create value.

<IR> of course does much more than this and, as I encourage businesses to at least incorporate elements of it, the benefits to internal processes and thinking become clear.

I hope the book plays a part in facilitating the uptake of <IR> thereby improving management practices.

Contents

Who This Book Is For

THIS BOOK IS FOR ALL THOSE CONCERNED about a specific organisation's performance (whether they be staff, providers of capital or other stakeholders) and all those who are concerned about improving the relationship between business (and other organisations), society and the environment.

Chief Sustainability Officers

By facilitating the uptake of <IR>, the book will help CSOs articulate the business case for their work, that is, the value it adds to the organisation. Instead of seeing their work as a cost, their colleagues will start to appreciate the benefits their work brings regardless of whether those benefits are directly monetary, measurable or difficult to quantify and not realisable in the short term. It will help them make their case in the language that CFOs understand.

CFOs, professional accounting bodies

CFOs, a product of the training of professional accounting bodies, have tended to: privilege information which can be quantified – preferably in monetary terms; focus on the short term; and ignore the impact that value creation and depletion of some of the capitals can have on long-term business success. All that must change for organisations that want to be around in the long term.

CEOs, senior managers and professional groupings for managers

CEOs and senior managers will gain a better understanding of how the various functions of an organisation contribute to organisational outcomes and value creation. For example, it will help human resources directors get people at the centre of strategy.

Non-Executive Directors and professional associations representing board directors

The book shows how <IR> can help organisations deliver on strategy and minimise risk.

University academics teaching and researching accounting and management

This book is a resource for teaching thereby facilitating the incorporation of <IR> and integrated thinking into the curriculum. It points to areas where further research is needed.

Students

The book highlights the link between accounting, accountability, reporting, management and performance helping to connect topics often covered in different subjects.

....

Foreword

by Paul Druckman
Chief Executive Officer of the
International Integrated Reporting Council (IIRC)

MY LONG-TERM VISION is a world in which integrated management and thinking are embedded within mainstream business practice in the public and private sectors, facilitated by Integrated Reporting '<IR>' as the corporate reporting norm. I believe the cycle of integrated thinking and reporting, resulting in efficient and productive capital allocation, will act as a force for financial stability and sustainability.

Today's corporate reporting landscape is more complex than ever before. Reporters and information users are bombarded by reams of information that do not provide a clear picture of a company's ability to create value in the long term. Companies are part of society and their strategy and business models must consider the context of their activities. Integrated reporting provides companies with an opportunity to tell their unique value creation story to providers of financial capital.

This book provides examples of the application of <IR> concepts and principles from leading report preparers and also includes a succinct and current overview of <IR>. I feel it is important to stress that we often place too much emphasis on the integrated report itself and not enough on the process and the paradigm shift that business and investors need to make to adopt <IR>.

This DōShort acknowledges that reflecting on the company's business model and its ability to create value is an important focal point. The more integrated thinking is embedded into an organisation's activities, the more naturally the connectivity of information flows into management reporting, analysis and decision-making. It also leads to better integration of the information systems that support internal and external reporting and communication, including the preparation of an integrated report.

I particularly appreciate the 'Before you report – things to consider' chapter. This is a quick guide to report preparers grappling with the first steps that are important to have in place prior to the preparation of an integrated report: 'Preparation', 'Getting buy-in' and 'Developing integrated thinking'. I believe that integrated thinking is at the core of Integrated Reporting – without an understanding of this concept we will not be able to achieve real integration in corporate reporting. This book takes a profound step in connecting this critical concept and its application to Integrated Reporting. The section dealing with 'fixing gaps in your integrated thinking' demonstrates that this concept challenges the current paradigm of business and poses some compelling reasons why companies may have identified these gaps through their reporting process.

This book is a significant contribution and a good source of learning about Integrated Reporting. It provides excellent examples of the evolution of corporate reporting to Integrated Reporting and will be of interest to a broad range of stakeholders. I am confident that Integrated Reporting does lend hope to the business–society nexus, the allocation of capital, and can make a lasting contribution to financial stability and sustainable development.

Paul Druckman
Chief Executive Officer, International Integrated Reporting Council

The IIRC's CEO, Paul Druckman chaired the Executive Board of the Prince's
Accounting for Sustainability (A4S; **www.accountingforsustainability.org**)
project and the FEE Sustainability Group (**www.fee.be/index.php?option
=com_content&view=article&id=39&Itemid=180**). Amongst many other
senior executive and non-executive roles, he was also Director of the
UK Financial Reporting Council (**www.frc.org.uk**) and President of the
Institute of Chartered Accountants in England and Wales (ICAEW; **www.
icaew.com**).

....

CHAPTER 1

Overview: What <IR> Is – and What It Is Not

THE INTERNATIONAL INTEGRATED REPORTING COMMITTEE (known since 2011 as the International Integrated Reporting Council) was formed in 2009 as an outcome of a high level meeting convened by HRH Prince of Wales to build on the work of the Prince's Accounting for Sustainability Project.[3] It was the culmination of various discussions, reports and initiatives including the 2009 King III Code of Governance for South Africa requiring from 2010 that companies listed on the Johannesburg Stock Exchange prepare Integrated Reports which integrate strategy, governance and sustainability.

The IIRC sees <IR> as an organisation's value creation story. It explains how the organisation will thrive in the short, medium and long term. It requires thinking beyond financial profit, thinking much more broadly about what creates value and what presents risk to value creation.

Companies cannot think of themselves as apart from society – they are part of it. And that needs to come through in their communication on value. PAUL DRUCKMAN, CEO IIRC[4]

<IR> is a new form of corporate reporting and whilst aimed primarily at providers of capital, the content is of interest to a broad range of stakeholders. Some still think of <IR> as simply bringing together financial

and sustainability performance information in one report. Indeed in recent research the GRI asked the question: 'Why did your organization start to combine financial and non-financial reporting?' (GRI, 2013a). It is much more than bringing together financial and sustainability reporting – and also much less than that. It does not replace either financial or sustainability reporting – both need to be in place for <IR>.

<IR> requires a fundamentally different way of thinking about what makes an organisation successful. It makes visible the organisation's reliance on a much broader set of capitals than financial capital. It requires a different way of working – working together, rather than in silos.

There are some common myths cropping up in the financial press and on blogs. Here are a few:

1. **<IR> makes sustainability reporting (and those that do it) redundant.** You cannot tell a comprehensive value creation story unless you have been identifying material sustainability risks and thinking about the benefits of your social, community and environmental investments.

2. **Disclosing strategy will present risks.** In fact <IR> will lead to a reduction in risk through more informed decision-making based on consideration of externalities and wider risks than might otherwise be the case.

3. **Preparing an integrated report means more work.** There should be nothing which needs to go in an integrated report which is not already gathered and prepared by a well-managed business. Much of the information is already communicated to providers of finance in an ad hoc way. Preparing an integrated report will

develop internal integrated thinking capacity. It is therefore an important investment. **The question business should be asking is whether they can afford *not* to do integrated reporting.**

If you call a report an integrated report and reference the International <IR> Framework you should comply with the requirements in bold italic type throughout this book unless reliable information is unavailable, legal prohibitions prevent disclosure or disclosure would cause significant competitive harm (see para. 1.17).[5]

"In the case of the unavailability of reliable information or specific legal prohibitions, an integrated report should:

- *Indicate the nature of the information that has been omitted*

- *Explain the reason why it has been omitted*

- *In the case of the unavailability of data, identify the steps being taken to obtain the information and the expected time frame for doing so."* (para. 1.18).

"An integrated report should include a statement from those charged with governance that includes:

- *An acknowledgement of their responsibility to ensure the integrity of the integrated report*

- *An acknowledgement that they have applied their collective mind to the preparation and presentation of the integrated report*

- *Their opinion or conclusion about whether the integrated report is presented in accordance with this Framework or, if it does not include such a statement, it should explain:*

- **What role those charged with governance played in its preparation and presentation**

- **What steps are being taken to include such a statement in future reports**

- **The time frame for doing so, which should be no later than the organization's third integrated report that references this Framework."** (para. 1.20)

In practice companies are currently responding to the momentum of <IR> in a variety of ways including: broadening the scope of their sustainability reports; putting additional information (such as specific International <IR> Framework content elements – see Chapter 7) in their annual report; and producing an additional report, but moving more sustainability disclosures online.

Who are integrated reports for?

Integrated reports are intended primarily for providers of capital including investors, shareholders or customers.

> *Integrated Reporting – embedding that concept of integration into business thinking and reporting processes – is essential for ensuring corporate reporting remains relevant to investors and plays a central role in their financial capital allocation decisions.*
> PAUL DRUCKMAN, CEO, IIRC

However, the International <IR> Framework recognises that a much broader group of stakeholders is interested in integrated reports.

I would like to see corporate reports being more about a true communication about the story of a business. This story should be more accessible to different stakeholders – that is, they can find what they want more easily. PAUL DRUCKMAN, CEO, IIRC

Indeed, Sasol's 2014 Annual Integrated Report, including the Chairman's Statement (p. 23) and the CEO's Review (p. 25) is addressed to 'stakeholders' rather than providers of capital. Sasol also talks about delivering value to stakeholders:

"Our shared values determine the way in which we determine and respond to business opportunities and challenges, and establish expectations about how we work with our colleagues, customers, shareholders, suppliers, partners, governments and the communities we serve." SASOL 2014 ANNUAL INTEGRATED REPORT,[6] p. 7

Sasol's discussion of the capitals, strategy and business model set out on the subsequent pages demonstrate a relatively mature stage of 'integrated thinking'.

Providers of capital come in all shapes and sizes. The CEO of one of the IIRC's smallest pilot businesses, bankmecu, a customer owned bank, commented:

We regard reporting as a critical element of our customer owned banking model and for these reasons we have integrated all the areas in which the business delivers value into our reporting process. We want our key stakeholders as well as those observers of our mutually owned business to understand clearly how we define, create, preserve and distribute value. DAMIEN WALSH,[7] CEO, BANKMECU

Who should prepare an integrated report?

Any type of organisation can prepare an integrated report, or adopt elements of the International <IR> Framework. Whilst the IIRC is aiming primarily at the for-profit private sector and most of the pilot companies are owned by investors and shareholders, other types of organisations would benefit from <IR>. (The benefits that preparing an integrated report can bring to companies and other types of organisations and their stakeholders are considered in Chapter 2.)

Take a legal firm where the predominance of partners are white men approaching retirement (perhaps with their eyes on the size of their pension funds), but with a vibrant, more diverse, younger staff wanting to feel they are making a contribution to society. This firm is engaged in ad hoc philanthropic, citizenship and diversity programmes and prepares a GRI sustainability report, but is still largely regarded by many stakeholders as just another greedy law firm. If this firm told customers how its various projects created value for the firm and society and linked its citizenship work with its strategy, vision and the type of law it practises, it would make its younger staff proud to work there. It would attract high calibre staff and customers who shared its vision and admired its approach (and perhaps others who wanted to be seen to share its vision). Telling its broader value creation story would give it a competitive advantage.

Universities exist for the public good and their long-term success depends on their ability to demonstrate it. Yet whilst they report outcomes, in terms of number and quality of publications, number of students educated, number of prizes, honorary degrees, etc., awarded, their record of reporting on material outcomes and the value they create, or their strategy to improve outcomes, is poor (Adams, 2013a).

Providers of finance to universities, their staff and students and national governments might expect them to report their contribution to solving the world's challenges and improving workforce skills. In reality, very few universities adequately incorporate these issues into strategy or have a comprehensive, joined-up approach to engaging stakeholders.[8] This is to their detriment and preparing first a sustainability report (which only a miniscule number of the world's universities currently do) and then an integrated report would help them improve process and refine strategy.

The not-for-profit (NFP) sector also stands to gain from <IR>. Like much of the public sector, the not-for-profit sector's means of creating value – for example, through volunteer resourced programmes – are often not made visible by compliance reporting. Yet reporting on project outcomes is critical to securing further funding. NFP's which demonstrate how *all* the resources (including volunteer resources) made available to them create value will likely benefit from a competitive advantage.

bankmecu[9] aims to appeal to customers through competitive interest rates and its reputation for responsible practices and social and environmental sustainability aiming 'to become the pre-eminent socially responsible banking brand in Australia'. Research[10] undertaken for bankmecu by Cannex, an independent Financial Services Research Group, has found that bankmecu customers (the bank's owners) are better off banking with bankmecu than the four major Australian banks. The benefits to bankmecu (and its customers) of telling its value creation story alongside demonstrating accountability for social, environmental and economic sustainability performance are obvious – they differentiate it from the big banks. This points to potential benefits of <IR> to smaller organisations.

Links to other reporting frameworks

The last decade has seen significant development in voluntary frameworks and both legislative and Stock Exchange requirements to increase corporate accountability for ESG issues and sustainability performance. This will undoubtedly continue and it would not be fruitful to list them all here. Suffice to say that <IR> does not conflict with any that I am aware of. I am also of the view that it does not reduce the need for them – a view which may or may not be shared by members of the IIRC.

Integrated reporting will help to bring sustainability reporting into the mainstream corporate reporting cycle. Sustainability reporting has been one of the great reporting innovations over the last twenty years – at its best it shows the essential relationship between a business, society, the economy and environment. It contains value-relevant information, yet is often disconnected from the financials. PAUL DRUCKMAN, CEO, IIRC

Financial reporting and sustainability reporting are essential to demonstrating accountability, sound management and governance. Whilst financial reporting is heavily regulated and audited, much of what comprises sustainability reporting is voluntary and unaudited. Globally, the extent and quality of sustainability reporting is woefully inadequate in both providing an account of performance to stakeholders and in assisting management to manage performance, a view informed by research, leadership and advisory work and sustainability report award judging. Sometimes there is a deliberate attempt to hide or deceive and sometimes there is a reluctance to disclose the activities the organisation is involved in which add value to society.

Integrated reporting is directed at providers of capital and sustainability reporting at a broader range of stakeholders. There is a need for both. Materiality for companies and for stakeholders is not necessarily aligned. IAN WOODS, HEAD OF ENVIRONMENT, SOCIAL AND GOVERNANCE RESEARCH, AMP CAPITAL

One detailed case study project involved comparing the portrayal of a multinational's sustainability performance in its own reports with that provided by a diverse variety of media outlets, academic literature and NGOs (Adams, 2004). The reports examined omitted material impacts to key stakeholder groups, misrepresented scientific literature and presented issues in a favourable light, not disclosing negative impacts. All in all, this amounts to a degree of incompleteness that would not be tolerated in financial reporting. Yet, what is at stake, when it comes to measuring and managing sustainability performance, for both business and their stakeholders seems to me to be at least as important, and arguably considerably more so, than measuring and reporting financial performance. Indeed we have witnessed many examples where poor sustainability reporting, performance and management processes have led to significant events (such as stakeholder action, a factory collapse, human rights abuses, a major pollution incident) with material financial consequences.

Preparing an integrated report requires sound financial and sustainability reporting processes (including stakeholder engagement processes). An integrated report cannot replace sustainability reporting. (Even if it could, there are strong business reasons why it shouldn't.) To be credible in the eyes of many, integrated reporters espousing broad notions of value creation and in demonstrating understanding of broader impacts on their business model, will need to be signatories to the UN Global Compact and apply the GRI sustainability reporting guidelines.

The practicalities of linking an organisation's various reporting processes in preparing an integrated report are discussed in Chapter 6.

....

CHAPTER 2

The Benefits of Preparing an Integrated Report

THE PROCESS OF DEVELOPING an integrated report brings real benefits. It highlights gaps in thinking, systems and processes. It involves thinking long term and collaboration across functions – or 'breaking down silos'. It ensures that material sustainability issues and risks get board-level attention.

UN Global Compact LEAD staff interviewed 20 participants about the Consultation Draft of the International Integrated Reporting <IR> Framework finding:

"The business case for sustainability can often be difficult to measure and share. Respondents affirm that integrated reporting has the potential to connect financial disclosures with sustainability in a way that makes them more relevant for a broader audience than would separate financial or sustainability reports, and that this greater level of integration of reporting practices encourages and supports the integration of sustainability in strategic planning, decision-making and operations." GLOBAL COMPACT LEAD SUBMISSION TO THE CONSULTATION DRAFT OF THE INTERNATIONAL INTEGRATED REPORTING <IR> FRAMEWORK[11]

When you think about it, getting your strategy right, understanding your business model, your risks and how you create value are amongst the most important determinants of success. The broader understanding of the business model, and particularly the consideration of the capitals, results in better risk identification.

I think business should be leading change to respond to climate change and social issues, but you need to find a business case to get traction. Risk is one key business issue, another is ability to execute strategy. Strategy is delivered by people, so staff retention and an engaged workforce is important in executing a strategy. A good reason for investing in your human capital is that your workforce becomes more productive – and more likely to meet your strategic goals. IAN WOODS, HEAD OF ENVIRONMENT, SOCIAL AND GOVERNANCE RESEARCH, AMP CAPITAL

Most innovations come from getting people from different functions and backgrounds together. The integrated thinking needed to produce an integrated report requires working together in setting your strategy and thinking about your business model.

There has been greater collaboration and cross-departmental discussion as a consequence of the integrated reporting project. The development of an illustration of bankmecu's business model for the report generated considerable inter-departmental searching and external testing considering vision and values, the strategic plan, customer-owned banking objectives, and departmental perspectives. The increased active involvement of the finance and accounting departments in the project and broader integrated reporting was an important internal aspect that challenges many businesses. DAMIEN WALSH, CEO, BANKMECU

HSBC's (http://www.hsbc.com/investor-relations) chief accounting officer Russell Picot has spoken[12] about the benefits of the integrated thinking[13] required for <IR> highlighting the role of <IR> in focusing discussion on the business model[14] and long-term strategic direction. Indeed, the need for integrated thinking is clear when reviewing HSBC's 2013 reports.[15] For further analysis of HSBC's reporting, see Chapter 7.

The top two benefits of <IR> are perhaps in:

1. Transforming decision-making processes in a way which aligns benefits to business, society and the environment. (A win-win all round – if it is done well.)

2. Better risk identification and mitigation. (A win for the company, its directors and the stakeholders it impacts.)

Realising these benefits is utterly dependent on a long-term time horizon and incentives are needed to facilitate this.

CEOs need long term incentives in their remuneration package. If companies don't think long term about ESG risks and their strategy, it catches up with them in the end. IAN WOODS, HEAD OF ENVIRONMENT, SOCIAL AND GOVERNANCE RESEARCH, AMP CAPITAL

The decision to change the nature of an organisation's reporting involves changes in what information is collected, how it is presented and ultimately, what aspects of an organisation's activities, processes and outcomes are made visible.

Integrated reporting will remove the marketing and pictorial reports from the front reception desk and ensure the critical information is linked to business outcomes. Integrated reporting

will enable better decision making and less trade-offs between the environment and finances. ALISON ROWE, GROUP EXECUTIVE DIRECTOR SUSTAINABILITY, FUJITSU

In <IR> the real changes will come through the emphasis on long-term thinking and much broader notions of creating value. A key person to influence transformative change in any organisation is the CFO – the holder of the purse strings.

The CFO needs to put a company on a path to sustainable performance. The CFO should not look short term by e.g. not investing in IT, talent etc. The modern CFO needs to think about performance over 10 years about the robustness of the business model to support long term value creation. This is not just about capex, it is more and more about reputation, attracting talent etc. The CFO needs to enable adaption of the business model to changes in attitude, regulation, availability of resources, etc. An integrated report leads with the idea that performance on all fronts leads to an enduring business model and performance. MARK JOINER, FORMER CFO, NATIONAL AUSTRALIA BANK

The requirement of the International <IR> Framework (IIRC, 2013a) to provide insight into the organisation's long-term strategy results in a significant benefit to many organisations. Nothing focuses the mind more than the decision to publicly disclose and integrated reporters will invest more in ensuring their strategy is fit for the long term.

In summary, <IR> brings benefits through:

- emphasising the need for long-term planning

- encouraging thinking about the business model in much broader terms than flows of money

- focusing on creating value across all six capitals

- developing a culture of collaboration, breaking down silos

- getting senior execs and the board involved in considering these issues.

The focus on long-term planning and collaboration across silos are fundamental prerequisites to embedding sustainability (see Adams, 2013b, in press).

....

CHAPTER 3

The Essential Ingredients of <IR>

THE TABLE BELOW PROVIDES A SUMMARY of the terms you need to be familiar with, each of which is discussed in the following chapters.

Essential 'ingredients' of <IR>

Fundamental concepts (even more important in determining what goes in the report than the guiding principles) See Chapter 4	• Value creation for the organisation and for others • The capitals • The value creation process
The six capitals (all the things a business needs to be successful) See Appendix	• financial capital • manufactured capital • intellectual capital • human capital • social and relationship capital • natural capital

Guiding principles (the principles that underpin the preparation of an integrated report informing its content and presentation) See Chapter 5	• Strategic focus and future orientation • Connectivity of information • Stakeholder relationships • Materiality • Conciseness • Reliability and completeness • Consistency and comparability
Integrated thinking (what's needed to develop an integrated report) See Chapter 6	*"Integrated thinking is the active consideration by an organization of the relationships between its various operating and functional units and the capitals that the organization uses or affects. Integrated thinking leads to integrated decision-making and actions that consider the creation of value over the short, medium and long term.'* (International <IR> Framework, Preface)
Content elements (what goes in the report) See Chapter 7	• Organisational overview & external environment • Governance • Business model • Risks and opportunities • Strategy and resource allocation • Performance • Outlook • Basis of preparation and presentation • General reporting guidance

CHAPTER 4

The Fundamental Concepts

THE INTERNATIONAL <IR> FRAMEWORK identifies three fundamental concepts: the value creation process; the capitals; and value creation for the organisation and others. These three concepts are interrelated in that you can't apply one in isolation of the others. Simply put, the capitals are inputs to the organisation's value creation process which creates value for the organisation and its stakeholders.

The value creation process

"Value is not created by or within an organization alone." (para. 2.2)

Paras 2.20 to 2.29 go on to discuss the value creation process. In order to understand their value creation process each reporting organisation will need to identify:

- which capitals it relies on;
- elements of the external environment relevant to its mission and vision;
- how the external environment and relationships with stakeholders influence its ability to create value;
- risks and opportunities;

- how the activities of the business convert the capitals into outputs (products, services, by-products and waste) and outcomes (the effects on the capitals).

Many organisations probably think they are doing all this already, but I'd be surprised to find any that, on making the decision to prepare an integrated report, did not find a value enhancing gap to fill.

Following the International <IR> Framework will enable the organisation to identify risks and opportunities and develop a strategy to mitigate or manage risks and take advantage of opportunities. Critical to all this is an understanding of performance on multiple dimensions – not just in financial terms.

The IIRC's Capitals Background Paper for <IR> (IIRC, 2013b; **http:// www.theiirc.org/wp-content/uploads/2013/03/IR-Background-Paper-Capitals.pdf**) considers 'value' in the context of the six capitals.[16] It recognises that organisations depend on all the capitals, not just financial capital, for their success and that some impacts on the capitals can only be reported on in narrative terms. It explicitly acknowledges that in their quest to create value overall, organisations might destruct or deplete the stock of one or more capitals in the process.

The capitals

"The capitals are stocks of value that are increased, decreased or transformed through the activities and outputs of the organization." (para. 2.16)

<IR> encourages organisations to think about the trade-offs between the capitals in the decision-making process and informs how individually and collectively the capitals contribute to the value creation process.

The capitals draw attention to the role of non-financial resources (often insufficiently recognised and acknowledged). The capitals concept is consistent with the emphasis in <IR> on thinking about long-term success, not just that in the short and medium terms. The pursuit of short-term success has been a key factor in, for example, environmental degradation and human rights abuses. This in turn has resulted in financial liabilities and reputation damage impacting on long-term success.

Organisations that take the challenge and change the way they think about their relationship with the capitals and the interrelationships between them will prosper in the long term.

The six capitals (financial, manufactured, intellectual, human, social and relationship and natural capital) are defined in the Appendix. The International <IR> Framework does intend that organisations report movements of the capitals under each of these six headings. The Framework also allows organisations to classify the capitals differently. In fact, the Framework explicitly acknowledges:

"While most organizations interact with all capitals to some extent, these interactions might be relatively minor or so indirect that they are not sufficiently important to include in the integrated report." (para. 2.19)

Rather, the capitals (which have been identified following extensive consultation and research) are intended to broaden thinking about the organisation's long-term value creation process and ensure that an organisation does not overlook a capital. In order to report performance on material ESG issues, organisations should prepare a sustainability report (or provide sustainability disclosures online).

Value creation for the organisation and others

The meaning attributed to 'value' and value to whom is critical in shifting the extent to which business, society and the environment co-exist in a mutually beneficial way. Is creating value about increasing shareholder wealth, improving the quality of lives of communities, enhancing our natural environment or all of these?

These tensions are to some extent drawn out in the IIRC's Value Creation Background Paper (IIRC, 2013d; **http://www.theiirc.org/wp-content/ uploads/2013/08/Background-Paper-Value-Creation.pdf**) prepared by EY with guidance from a multi-stakeholder expert steering committee. The International <IR> Framework acknowledges both value created for stakeholders and value created for the organisation itself (see para. 2.4). The latter results in financial returns to providers of capital. An organisation's external context, relationships, business activities and outputs all have an impact on value creation.

The value an organisation creates (or depletes) for others can have an impact on long-term value creation for the organisation and its providers of capital (see para. 2.5).

A business–society relationship characterised by trust and mutual advantage is critical to the long-term success of companies. The extent to which any individual organisation transforms itself and contributes to transforming this relationship will depend on how they articulate what value creation means to them and the way in which stakeholder concerns influence 'value'. Also important is the extent to which the senior executive and board shift towards longer-term thinking.

The IIRC's Value Creation Background Paper considers value from the perspective of the organisation and specifically from the perspective of providers of financial capital in noting (p. 11):

"Providers of financial capital equate value creation with the potential for future cash flows and sustainable financial returns, but this also takes into account the importance and limitations of different forms of capital for value creation."

From this perspective then, the six capitals might only be considered in the <IR> process to the extent that they were thought to lead to measurable impact on financial returns for providers of capital. In the context of climate change it is surely clear that this is unacceptable. Global failure to reduce emissions, and so avoiding the planet becoming uninhabitable to people, including providers of capital, would mean zero financial returns. At points in time prior to this, the impact of climate change on financial returns to providers of capital of any one particular company might be very difficult to predict. Does this mean that organisations do not need to report their emissions? Of course, they should.

The IIRC's Value Creation Background Paper acknowledged that stakeholder concerns and actions can influence financial returns and that the impacts may not be immediate or direct. In fact, the impact of stakeholder actions and concerns may not be measureable in financial terms for a long time, if at all. Nevertheless, countless examples have demonstrated that they present a considerable risk if not addressed. It is in a company's interest to recognise the importance of 'stakeholder relationships' (a Guiding Principle of <IR> – see Chapter 5) to creating value.

Sasol and Vodocom provide examples. The Sasol 2014 Annual Integrated Report[17] sets out the contribution that each stakeholder group makes to creating value (pp. 38–39). Similarly Vodocom's 2012 Integrated Report[18] sets out 'why it's important for us to engage' with each stakeholder group (pp. 14–15).

The IIRC's Value Creation Background Paper (IIRC, 2013d, p. 11) nevertheless goes on to say:

"Integrated reports should enable providers of financial capital to assess whether, to what extent and how an organization's use of, and outcomes for, all of the capitals adds to financial value."
[Emphasis added]

This could be interpreted by some as meaning business as usual – if you can't measure it in monetary terms, it's not important.

Accountants could do much more than they have to date been inclined to measure the impacts of corporate business models across all six capitals and of stakeholder actions. <IR> could play an important role in this. But telling accountants, who play an important role in corporate reporting, that they should only include impacts if their financial value can be measured is unlikely to encourage lateral thinking. **It comes down to how your organisation defines value.**

The message is somewhat different on p. 14:

"When reporting on value, an organization may. . . draw a boundary around elements and interactions that are most relevant to their business model and strategy, and therefore to the way in which the organization expects to create value over time. The boundary should be disclosed together with any significant assumptions and estimates made by management

in its disclosures about value creation, so that intended users understand the limitations of the connections that it is possible for the organization to make, given that some of them might be outside its sphere of knowledge, or might not yet be apparent."

This assumes that companies a) have a desire to be accountable and b) have the know-how to report in this way. It also points to the need for external assurance if reports are to be credible.

To a very large extent, how companies respond will depend on how corporate managers, boards and report users really believe their thinking needs to shift longer term.

The International <IR> Framework and Background papers do quite a good job of establishing the need for longer-term thinking. But is it enough to shift the focus of reporting far enough for the relationship between organisations, society and the environment to improve so that all can prosper long term? Time will tell and the onus is as much on individual companies to define what they mean by value and to whom.

I am reminded of Ruth Hines's (1991) article titled 'On Valuing Nature' in an accounting journal. It starkly demonstrated the limitations of accounting to measure the value of nature and relationships and finished with the words:

"It is in the name of Net Profit, Budget Surplus and Gross National Product that the natural environment in which we all co-exist is being destroyed. Those who speak this language have more social power to influence thinking and actions than they perhaps realise, or utilise."

Since that time the Global Reporting Initiative (GRI) and the International Integrated Reporting Council have emerged. The GRI has played a part in change. With its appeal to investors and corporate boards the IIRC can help accelerate change.

In summary, whilst not an explicit requirement of the International <IR> Framework, in order to credibly articulate their valuation story, organisations should:

- disclose how they define value and the relevance of stakeholder views and the six capitals to their concept of value

- disclose what steps they have taken to maximise value creation according to their definition

- seek external assurance to demonstrate that they are working to create value as they define it

I am confident that the organisations that prosper long term will be those that listen to their stakeholders and define value broadly in terms of all six capitals.

....

CHAPTER 5

The Guiding Principles

THE INTERNATIONAL <IR> FRAMEWORK includes the following guiding principles:

- Strategic focus and future orientation

- Connectivity of information

- Stakeholder relationships

- Materiality

- Conciseness

- Reliability and completeness

- Consistency and comparability

The Framework acknowledges that there are tensions between guiding principles (the obvious area for tension being between conciseness and completeness) and calls for judgement to be used in applying them. That is exactly why they are 'principles' – they are there to guide and to be applied with judgement.

The Framework goes on to specify what an integrated report should look like if the principles are appropriately applied. That is, an integrated report should:

- *"provide insight into the organization's strategy, and how that relates to its ability to create value in the short, medium and long term and to its use of and effects on the capitals"* (para. 3.3 – strategic focus and future orientation);

- *"show a holistic picture of the combination, inter-relatedness and dependencies between the factors that affect the organization's ability to create value over time"* (para. 3.6 – connectivity of information);

- *"provide insight into the nature and quality of the organization's relationships with its key stakeholders, including how and to what extent the organization understands, takes into account and responds to their legitimate needs and interests"* (para. 3.10 – stakeholder relationships);

- *"disclose information about matters that substantively affect the organization's ability to create value over the short, medium and long term"* (para. 3.17 – materiality);

- *"be concise"* (para. 3.36 – conciseness);

- *"include all material matters, both positive and negative, in a balanced way and without material error"* (para. 3.39 – reliability and completeness);

- *"be presented (a) on a basis that is consistent over time and, (b) in a way that enables comparison with other organizations to the extent it is material to the organization's own ability to create value in the short, medium and long term"* (para. 3.54 – consistency and comparability).

Chapter 6 discusses how the **materiality** approach for sustainability reporting can be adapted/extended for <IR> and also how the guiding principle of **stakeholder relationships** can be fulfilled. **Connectivity** is discussed in Chapter 7.

Conciseness, reliability and completeness and consistency and comparability are relatively self-explanatory. Whilst annual reports and sustainability reports have tended to be voluminous rather than concise, preparers of both reports *should* be familiar with the need for both '**reliability and completeness**' and '**consistency and comparability**'. These principles are relatively easily applied in financial reporting where approaches are mandated and results required to be audited.

The specification that negative as well as positive material issues should be disclosed is welcome. Many sustainability reports, where there are limited mandatory requirements, have omitted material negative impacts making them incomplete (see the discussion in Chapter 6).

Achieving comparability across organisations on non-financial and sustainability performance is more challenging due to the varied quality and extent of non-financial and sustainability reporting. The principles of reliability and comparability also apply to G4 (GRI, 2013b, p. 18; **https:// www.globalreporting.org/reporting/g4/Pages/default.aspx**).

In fulfilling the requirement that organisations provide insight into their '**strategic focus and future orientation**' it is important to demonstrate that the strategy set out in the report is achievable. This can be done by describing how the past has led to the current strategic focus and highlighting key financial and non-financial performance indicators that demonstrate that strategy has been achieved in the past (see Chapter 7 for examples).

CHAPTER 6

Before You Report – Things to Consider/Do

THERE ARE A NUMBER OF STEPS that need to be taken and decisions made before you start to prepare your integrated report. These fall into three broad categories:

- preparation

- getting buy in

- developing integrated thinking.

Ten steps to <IR>

Preparation

1. **Develop sustainability reporting.** If you are not already preparing a sustainability report, or collecting and disclosing material social, environmental and economic information, do this first. Sign up to the UN Global Compact (**http://www.globalcompact.org**) and follow the GRI Guidelines (GRI, 2013b).

2. **Assess the adequacy of the stakeholder engagement processes to identify issues relevant to preparing an integrated report.** Stakeholder engagement processes are an essential component

of preparing a quality sustainability report. In some organisations these processes focus on identifying material social, environmental and economic sustainability issues. In others they are much broader and seek to identify issues that might impact on the organisation's ability to create value over time.

Getting buy in

3. **Get senior management buy in.** If the decision to prepare an integrated report has not come from the top, start where you think you will get most support. Influential people will likely be the CEO, the CFO, the Company Secretary and perhaps the person responsible for strategic planning. A board member with a particular interest in the aims of <IR> may have influence. The Chief Sustainability Officer/Head of Sustainability may have already started to think about sustainability in terms of value creation.

4. **Get board buy in.** Board buy in is important not least because of the requirement that an integrated report provide insights into strategy and identify who and/or which governance body is responsible for its content. If you have some keen board members, you may get board buy in before all the senior management commit.

5. **Get agreement on your reporting package.** You will need to consider whether you will adopt the framework in full right away, which requires you to produce an identified integrated report, or adopt elements of it in stages. Will you prepare a separate integrated report, include (some of) the <IR> framework content elements at the front of your annual review and/or include some

in your sustainability report? How will you make information available to key stakeholders? You will need to consider the extent to which you will make greater use of online reporting to disclose non-material information, whether you will use an app, etc.

Developing integrated thinking

6. **Determine material issues.** Determining material issues for <IR> involves both engaging with stakeholders and engaging your senior management team. The process is discussed in more detail later in the chapter.

7. **Get agreement on your business model and its relationship with the six capitals.** When you start discussing your business model with your senior team, you may well find that that there are as many different views about key aspects of it as there are people in the room. Some will need to be encouraged to think more broadly than flows of money.

8. **Develop your value creation story.** Your value creation story should be expressed in terms of all six capitals and should connect with your business model (see Chapter 7).

9. **Articulate your strategy.** Strategy should be articulated in a way that connects with your value creation story.

10. **Check for connectivity of information.** Connectivity of information both within your integrated report and across your reports and other communications is critical to sending a strong, credible message. It is addressed in Chapter 7.

Fixing gaps in your integrated thinking

Developing integrated thinking is a bit of an iterative process. You won't get it right first time and once you start reporting you will identify gaps in your thinking. And it is not until you report that some gaps will be noticed. Fixing the gaps (which you should expect to do only temporarily because it is a continual challenge) requires understanding why they occur. Likely reasons include:

- **A belief that anything of value to business has to be measureable in monetary terms.** This can be hard to shake and the education and training of accountants tends not to challenge it. The good news is that research shows that younger people are seeking to work for organisations that are socially responsible, practise sustainability and are ethical. Those whose responsibilities involve creating value through non-financial means need to clearly articulate the value created to the organisation and its stakeholders by their initiatives.

- **Organisational structures which predate the complexity of the contemporary, complex and globalised business environment.** There are still an abundance of organisations with thriving silos. If organisations are to thrive they need to get better at working across these silos by developing formal and informal communication channels and networks.

- **Territorial and hierarchical (i.e. 'masculine') leadership styles.** These are difficult to change. Looking for different leadership styles when recruiting new managers can shift the culture – as can increasing diversity.

- **The predominance of leaders who lack a 'moral compass'**

and hence authenticity. If this applies you may well have bigger issues to deal with than fixing gaps in integrated thinking (see Adams, 2013b).

What is your value creation story?

Chapter 1 discussed how telling your organisation's value creation story could itself add value to different types of organisations. Chapter 4 considered the meaning of value and value to whom.

Integrated reporting is where an organisation explains how it is going to create value. It is a concise communication of value. It explains how a company will be a viable thriving entity in the short, medium and long term. It is not just about financial profit.
PAUL DRUCKMAN, CEO, IIRC

Remember that your vision is an important starting point in telling your value creation story. The vision is the starting point for an organisation's strategy. It will shape what value means.

An example is provided by the Chartered Institute of Management Accountants' (CIMA) 2013 annual report[19] which includes a section on 'Creating Value Together' identifying a number of 'resources' such as employees, students, members, employers etc and explaining how they fit into the business model and create value to the organisation. Another example of an inclusive, 'integrated' vision is Unilever's (see next section).

Thinking about your business model more broadly

Thinking about your business model and discussing it is a good idea regardless of whether you are preparing an integrated report. The IIRC's Business Model Background Paper for <IR> (IIRC, 2013c; **http://www.theiirc.org/resources-2/framework-development/background-papers/**) provides some frameworks for those discussions. It encourages companies to think of the business model as its 'chosen system of inputs, business activities, outputs and outcomes that aims to create value'. An excellent example of a business model depicted in this way is in the professional accounting body ACCA's 2013 annual report.[20]

Try asking your senior team to identify your main inputs, activities, outputs and outcomes: you may well find they come up with different things and certainly different priorities. Hopefully, they will at least all be thinking beyond traditional narrow concepts of business models being about how an organisation makes money. Such narrow views will not make for long-term business success.

Business inputs need to be considered in terms of people, infrastructure, relationships, natural resources, etc., as well as funds. For example, people are critical to a professional services organisation but very often reporting focuses predominantly on financial inputs perhaps with a few statements along the lines of 'our staff are our biggest asset' thrown in. Companies should be able to articulate how they nurture that resource and add value to it.

Stakeholders are interested in the impact of business inputs and activities on a range of capitals (see Appendix). This includes the impact on the environment, employees and communities. But outcomes that can't be measured in dollars or pounds are often seen as outside the business model. They are in fact an important part of it.

Integrating sustainability involves acknowledging its relevance to the business model and value add to business outcomes. Identifying and managing ESG risks is important to value protection. CARLOTA GARCIA-MANAS, HEAD OF RESEARCH, EIRIS

Inputs are owned by society and outcomes impact on all of us. Articulating what your business contributes to society is therefore critical to your success. Do you have a process to ensure that you give due weight to trade-offs across the six capitals in your decision-making? If not, develop one.

Companies need to critically challenge their understanding of the complex relationship between all of their inputs, activities, outputs and outcomes and find innovative ways of reporting on their business model. The process should take account of stakeholder views and recognise that creating value for one stakeholder group may diminish it for another.

Unilever (an IIRC pilot company) have recognised that thinking about your business model more broadly starts with your vision. Theirs is:

"Double the size of the business, whilst reducing our environmental footprint and increasing our positive social impact." UNILEVER'S 2013 ANNUAL REPORT,[21] p. 1

Their goal of 'sustainable living' and their 'people' are central to the business model (depicted in Figure 1). Their Sustainable Living Plan focuses on: improving health and well-being; reducing environmental impact; and enhancing livelihoods (pp. 22 and 23).

FIGURE 1. Unilever's Business Model

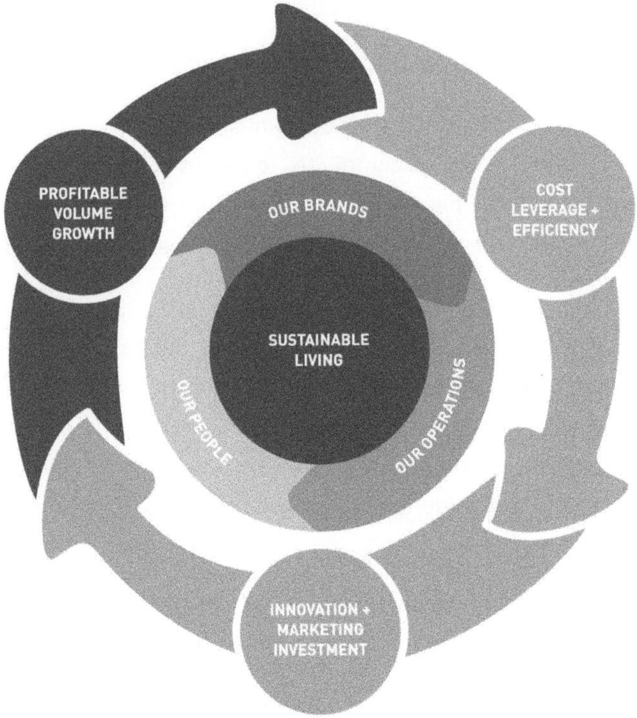

SOURCE: Unilever's 2013 Annual Report and Accounts, p. 9 (http://www.unilever.com/ investorrelations/annual_reports/AnnualReportandAccounts2013/)

Business is part of society and needs to play its part in shaping society, providing employment and opportunities to people and in protecting the world we are caretaking for the future generations.
RAY BREMNER, PRESIDENT AND CEO, UNILEVER JAPAN

Determining material issues

Over the last few years, processes for the determination of material issues for sustainability reporting have become increasingly broad in terms of the issues that are considered relevant. Examples include recent sustainability reports of Fuji Xerox Australia and the Royal Bank of Scotland (discussed below). *The Materiality Report* (Forstater et al., 2006) demonstrates the benefits of linking the materiality process with strategy development, performance management and creating value. Its Materiality Framework defines material issues as those that could make a major difference to an organisation's performance. Quotes in the *Materiality Report* from executives in leading organisations indicate that practice was already heading in the direction of integrating materiality in financial and sustainability reporting. This one, for example, was provided by Karin Ireton, then with Anglo American (p. 25):

> *"We are trying to align boundaries and definitions of materiality between financial and sustainability reporting, but it is at an early stage. I would say there is currently more conversation than alignment. . . This is one of the priorities at the moment – to try to drive this in a more integrated and embedded fashion – everything we do is looking for ways that this is not an add-on process, it is integral to the way we do business."*

The GRI's G4 guidelines define the Materiality Principle more narrowly than it is sometimes applied in sustainability reports as:

> *"The report should cover Aspects that:*
>
> * *Reflect the organisation's significant economic, environmental and social impacts; or*

* *Substantively influence the assessments and decisions of stakeholders."* GRI, 2013, p. 17

Economic impacts refer to impacts on economies and the economic situation of stakeholders rather than the financial performance of the organisation.

Stakeholders are defined in G4 as follows:

"Stakeholder can include those invested in the organization as well as those who have other relationships to the organisation." GRI, 2013, p. 16 [Emphasis added]

With respect to identification of material issues the Fuji Xerox Australia 2013 sustainability report, for example, includes 'responding to digitisation through innovation' and 'being customer centric' in the top ten material issues. Fuji Xerox Australia's provider of capital, parent company Fuji Xerox Co Ltd, is included in the list of stakeholders and the company took steps in 2013 to involve staff in the final prioritisation of material issues.

The RBS Group's RBS Sustainability Review 2013[22] identifies customer trust and culture and ethical conduct as its top two 'stakeholder issues' (p. 10). A distinguishing feature of the 2012 report was the breadth of issues included in the materiality approach. In 2013 a wider range of stakeholders were consulted (page 9), including the Board level Group Sustainability Committee. Notably the Board level Group Sustainability Committee met with 26 advocacy groups during 2013. The scope of issues raised by them was again broad including customer trust, governance and accountability, regulatory reform and compliance alongside the usual issues which arise in a sustainability report stakeholder engagement process such as human rights, diversity and inclusion.

The involvement of senior managers is an important step in developing integrated thinking and determining material issues.

The Fuji Xerox Australia Sustainability Report 2013[23] states:

"Like many organisations, embedding sustainability in how we plan, manage and measure our business remains a key challenge and requires continual refinement. Our goal is to integrate the voice of stakeholders in what we call the strategic rhythm of the business.

In 12/13 we took steps towards this by workshopping the final prioritisation step of our materiality process with a diverse selection of employees from across the business. This allowed our people to better understand how material issues are identified and the nature of the issues themselves. It also created an appetite for the rich qualitative insights from our materiality process to be shared more broadly. This work will be carried forward in 13/14:

- *our stakeholder materiality matrix will be refined alongside the corporate risk register, and both will form part of our annual planning process*

- *a framework will be developed to assist the management and measurement of our material issues across the business*

- *voice of stakeholder will be shared with members of our leadership and management team."*

Sasol and Unilever, both of whom have made a commitment to integrated reporting, highlight key financial and non-financial indicators together and right up front in their reports (sending a strong signal about the importance of both):

- **Sasol 2014 Annual Integrated Report** (http://www.sasol.com/ investor-centre/publications/integrated-report-1): Trend data plus targets and the dates targets are to be achieved by are provided for key financial and non-financial indicators on pp. 4–5. Non-financial indicators cover safety and equity issues.

- **Unilever 2013 annual report** (http://www.unilever.com/images/ Unilever_AR13_tcm13-383757.pdf): The report highlights six financial and six non-financial indicators right up front in the report on pp. 2–3. The non-financial indicators include both social and environmental sustainability issues which are material to Unilever and its stakeholders.

....

CHAPTER 7

How to Report

THE HARD WORK, the integrated thinking and changing the way you view things, was outlined in Chapter 6. Now you just have to put it all down on paper, or digitally.

There are a number of resources that can be used to identify further examples of good integrated reporting. These include:

- The IIRC's Emerging Integrated Reporting Database.[24] The database allows identification of examples of reporting by content element, sector and geographic region.

- The **CorporateRegister.com** online database of company reports. The Corporate Register Reporting Awards[25] now include a category for Integrated Reports.

- PWC (2013). The value creation journey: A survey of JSE Top-40 companies' integrated reports (**http://www.pwc.co.za/en_ZA/za/ assets/pdf/integrated-reporting-august-2013.pdf**). Analysis of the Johannesburg Stock Exchanges top 40 companies' Integrated Reports.

- EY (2013) Excellence in Integrated Reporting Awards (**http://www. ey.com/Publication/vwLUAssets/EYs_Excellence_in_Integrated_ Reporting_Awards_2013/$FILE/EY%20Excellence%20in%20 Integrated%20Reporting.pdf**). Surveys integrated reports from

South Africa's top 100 companies and top 10 public entities providing feedback on the reports of the top 10 companies.

Highly thought of Integrated Reports from these sources include: CIMA (see Chapter 6), CPA Australia (good coverage of challenges and future focus), Novo Nordisk (includes long-term financial, social and environmental targets), Sasol (see Chapters 1, 4, 6 and 7), Standard Bank Group (contribution to South African social and economic development), Takeda Pharmaceutical Company (links Corporate Social Responsibility and sustainability practices to their value creation process) and Vodocom (clearly sets out their value creation process).

What your report needs to include – The content elements

The content elements guide what goes in your integrated report. They are:

- Organizational overview & external environment

- Governance

- Business model

- Risks and opportunities

- Strategy and resource allocation

- Performance

- Outlook

- Basis of presentation

- General reporting guidance

To comply with the International <IR> Framework an integrated report should answer the following questions:

"What does the organization do and what are the circumstances under which it operates?" (para. 4.4)

"How does the organization's governance structure support its ability to create value in the short, medium and long term?" (para. 4.8)

"What is the organization's business model?" (para. 4.10)

What are the specific risks and opportunities that affect the organization's ability to create value over the short, medium and long term, and how is the organization dealing with them?" (para. 4.23)

"Where does the organization want to go and how does it intend to get there?" (para. 4.27)

"To what extent has the organization achieved its strategic objectives for the period and what are its outcomes in terms of effects on the capitals?" (para. 4.30)

"What challenges and uncertainties is the organization likely to encounter in pursuing its strategy, and what are the potential implications for its business model and future performance?" (para. 4.34)

"How does the organization determine what matters to include in the integrated report, and how are such matters quantified or evaluated?" (para. 4.40)

This should be relatively straightforward if you've done the integrated thinking work outlined in earlier chapters.

An additional report or an amended annual/sustainability report?

"An integrated report may be either a standalone report or be included as a distinguishable, prominent or accessible part of another report or communication." (para. 1.15)

To date, and as noted earlier and demonstrated by research (GRI, 2013a), a variety of practices in nomenclature and format for integrated reporting have developed during the process of developing the International <IR> Framework. The International <IR> Framework requires integrated reports to be a separately identifiable communication.

Integrated reporting is directed at providers of capital and sustainability reporting at a broader range of stakeholders. There is a need for both. Materiality for companies and for stakeholders is not necessarily aligned. Generally 6–8 pages of information for investors and other stakeholder groups is enough. Companies need to think about different types of reports for different audiences and make them short and relevant to that audience. IAN WOODS, HEAD OF RESEARCH, AMP CAPITAL

HSBC have said that their integrated report will be additional to their existing reporting package.

Sasol's 2014 Annual Integrated Report (**http://www.sasol.com/investor-centre/publications/integrated-report-1**) includes a helpful introductory section that briefly summarises the key purposes of the report along with the annual financial statements, Form 20-F and the 'sustainable development' report, clearly differentiating between the various reports and the frameworks and regulations which apply to each.

Remember that 'conciseness', one of the Guiding Principles of <IR> covered in Chapter 3, is key.

Achieving connectivity of information

Connectivity is something to keep a check on throughout the reporting process. The following bits of information need to connect:

- Content sections of an integrated report

- Relationship between past performance and future strategy

- Six capitals

- Integrated report and other corporate reports

To do this well, you need a culture of collaboration and communication processes which cross functional silos. These can be developed with time. It may require fixing the reasons why gaps in information occur:

- Belief that anything of value to business has to be measureable in monetary terms

- Organisational structures that predate the complexity of the contemporary, complex and globalised business environment

- Territorial and hierarchical (i.e. 'masculine') leadership styles

- The predominance of leaders who lack a 'moral compass' and hence authenticity

A review of HSBC's annual (**http://www.hsbc.com/investor-relations/ financial-results**) and sustainability (**http://www.hsbc.com/citizenship/ sustainability**) reports reveals that there is much work to be done in terms of connectivity of information. The reports portray an organisation where integrated thinking is in its infancy. Indeed, the IIRC's pilot programme 2012 yearbook (**http://www.theiirc.org/wp-content/uploads/Yearbook _2012/sources/indexPop.htm**) notes HSBC's difficulty in demonstrating connectivity in creating value whilst only the Finance and Sustainability teams are involved in <IR>. This indicates that there is a need for integrated thinking to involve a greater number of functional areas.

The 'business model' is discussed (p. 13 of its 2013 annual report) in narrow terms focusing on financial capital with a lack of reference to broader capitals. It is not connected with the statement on 'how we manage our business' in the 2012 sustainability report (page 5).

The limited information on people or capital in the business model is particularly at odds with a service organisation. And while there is reference to the need to build relationships with customers and suppliers and invest in communities for future growth (page 10) this is not explicitly linked with the business model (page 13) or the discussion on how the bank creates value (page 9).

Reporting the processes of developing this integrated thinking and determining material issues would lend credibility to what is reported.

Where reporting needs to go

There is always more that can be done to improve the quality and relevance of corporate reporting and it is worth having an agreed plan as to how you would like to see your reporting develop over the next few years.

Paul Druckman, CEO IIRC, offered this:

*I would highlight the following areas where I think we need to see
more progress:*

1. *A better articulation of strategy and ensuring that this is
    reflected throughout the reporting process, not just in one
    place in the report.*

2. *A bringing to life of the concept of 'connectivity' – the
    recognition of all the interconnected pieces across the
    business – which is such an essential part of <IR>.*

3. *A real focus on conciseness – currently, many businesses
    are working on bringing together information. A reduction
    in volume should flow from the application of Integrated
    Reporting principles.*

Of ongoing concern to me, having read hundreds of corporate reports,
is the level of accountability and degree of completeness with respect to
material social and environmental impacts.

Not enough organisations are making the link between accountability
and reputation, but their stakeholders, including increasingly providers
of capital, are. PWC (2013) makes additional suggestions has to how
reporting might develop.

....

CHAPTER 8

A Word on Assurance of Integrated Reports

THERE ARE DIVERSE VIEWS on the assurance of integrated reports and agreement on best practice is yet to develop.

What is clear is that an external assurance process can add significant value to management as data collection systems, internal control, reporting and decision-making processes evolve to meet the demands of <IR>.

In addition to evolving systems and processes, internal dynamics will shift: there may be tussles for ownership of parts of the processes, which external input, by way of an assurance provider management letter, may help to resolve.

A more proactive response to meeting this particular need might be to get this sort of guidance through involving an external expert as a 'critical friend' in internal planning meetings.

The credibility of integrated reports depends to a significant extent on the processes rather than the accuracy of numbers (which readers would expect to be audited through a financial and sustainability report assurance process). Readers of integrated reports will want answers to questions such as:

- How was the business model developed? Is it complete?

- What is the extent of cooperation across senior management (and silos)?

- Have key stakeholders been consulted and senior management involved in determining material issues?

- Is there a link ('connectivity') between the vision, strategy, business model, inputs, outputs and outcomes?

- Is the strategy achievable given externalities, the business model, the resources available and performance to date?

Sustainability assurance processes may address some of these issues, but not all.

The IIRC's Assurance on <IR> (**http://www.theiirc.org/resources-2/ assurance/**): an exploration of issues (IIRC 2014) discusses an assurance approach for the principles and content elements of <IR> and some methodological issues in assurance for <IR> primarily from the perspective of financial auditing. It seems somewhat odd that it compares materiality for <IR>, the most important, game-changing components of which are non-financial, with materiality in financial reporting. The approach used in some sustainability reports is arguably much more appropriate given that they deal almost exclusively with non-financial issues..

....

Categorisation and Description of The Capitals

THE CAPITALS ARE DEFINED in para. 2.15 of the International <IR> Framework as follows:

> *"For the purpose of this Framework, the capitals are categorized and described as follows:*
>
> Financial capital – *The pool of funds that is:*
>
> - *available to an organization for use in the production of goods or the provision of services*
>
> - *obtained through financing, such as debt, equity or grants, or generated through operations or investments.*
>
> Manufactured capital – *Manufactured physical objects (as distinct from natural physical objects) that are available to an organization for use in the production of goods or the provision of services, including:*
>
> - *buildings*
>
> - *equipment*
>
> - *infrastructure (such as roads, ports, bridges, and waste and water treatment plants).*

Manufactured capital is often created by other organizations, but includes assets manufactured by the reporting organization for sale or when they are retained for its own use.

Intellectual capital – *Organizational, knowledge-based intangibles, including:*

- *intellectual property, such as patents, copyrights, software, rights, and licences*

- *'organizational capital' such as tacit knowledge, systems, procedures and protocols*

Human capital – *People's competencies, capabilities and experience, and their motivations to innovate, including their:*

- *alignment with and support for an organization's governance framework, risk management approach, and ethical values*

- *ability to understand, develop and implement an organization's strategy*

- *loyalties and motivations for improving processes, goods and services, including their ability to lead, manage and collaborate.*

Social and relationship capital – *The institutions and the relationships within and between communities, groups of stakeholders and other networks, and the ability to share information to enhance individual and collective well-being. Social and relationship capital includes:*

- *shared norms, and common values and behaviours*

- *key stakeholder relationships, and the trust and willingness to engage that an organization has developed and strives to build and protect with external stakeholders*

- *intangibles associated with the brand and reputation that an organization has developed.*

- an organization's social licence to operate.

Natural capital – *All renewable and non-renewable environmental resources and processes that provide goods or services that support the past, current or future prosperity of an organization. It includes:*

- *air, water, land, minerals and forests*

- *biodiversity and eco-system health."*

References

Adams, C.A. 2004. The ethical, social and environmental reporting – performance portrayal gap *Accounting, Auditing and Accountability Journal* (Volume 17, Issue 5): 731–757. Author's copy available at http:// drcaroladams.net/the-ethical-social-and-environmental-reporting-performance-portrayal-gap/

Adams, C.A. 2013a. Sustainability reporting and performance management in universities: challenges and benefits *Sustainability Accounting, Management and Policy Journal* (Volume 4, Issue 3): 384–392. Author's copy available at http://drcaroladams.net/sustainability-reporting-and-performance-management-in-universities-challenges-and-benefits/

Adams, C.A. 2013b. The role of leadership and governance in transformational change towards sustainability. *Global Responsibility* (Issue 9). Author's copy available at http://drcaroladams.net/the-role-of-leadership-and-governance-in-transformational-change-towards-sustainability/

Adams, C A (in press) The International Integrated Reporting Council: a call to action *Critical Perspectives on Accounting*, DOI 10.1016/j.cpa.2014.07.001. Author's copy available at http://drcaroladams.net/the-international-integrated-reporting-council-a-call-to-action/

EY (2013) Excellence in Integrated Reporting Awards. http://www.ey.com/Publication/vwLUAssets/EYs_Excellence_in_Integrated_Reporting_Awards_2013/$FILE/EY%20Excellence%20in%20Integrated%20Reporting.pdf

Forstater, M., Zadek, S., Evans, D., Knight, A., Sillanpää, M., Tuppen, C. and Warris, A.-M. 2006. The Materiality Report: Aligning Strategy, Performance and Reporting. AccountAbility in association with BT Group and Lloyds Register Quality Assurance. http://www.accountability.org/images/content/0/8/088/The%20Materiality%20Report.pdf

GRI. 2013a. The Sustainability Content of Integrated Reports – A Survey of Pioneers. https://www.globalreporting.org/resourcelibrary/GRI-IR.pdf

GRI. 2013b. G4 Sustainability Reporting Guidelines Part 1 Reporting Principles and Standard Disclosures. https://www.globalreporting.org/reporting/g4/Pages/default.aspx

Hines, R. 1991. On valuing nature. Accounting Auditing and Accountability Journal (Volume 4, Issue 3): 27–29.

IIRC. 2013a. International <IR> Framework. http://theiirc.org

IIRC. 2013b. Capitals Background Paper for <IR>. http://www.theiirc.org/wp-content/uploads/2013/03/IR-Background-Paper-Capitals.pdf

IIRC. 2013c. Business Model Background Paper for <IR>. http://www.theiirc.org/wp-content/uploads/2013/03/Business_Model.pdf

IIRC. 2013d. Value Creation Background Paper for <IR>. http://www.theiirc.org/wp-content/uploads/2013/08/Background-Paper-Value-Creation.pdf

IIRC. 2014. Assurance on <IR>: and exploration of issues. Available at http://www.theiirc.org/resources-2/assurance/

PWC. 2013. The value creation journey: A survey of JSE Top-40 companies' integrated reports. http://www.pwc.co.za/en_ZA/za/assets/pdf/integrated-reporting-august-2013.pdf

Resources

SEE CHAPTER 7 FOR A LIST of resources for identifying good <IR> examples and analysis of them.

The International Integrated Reporting Council at **http://theiirc.org**

Towards Sustainable Business at **http://drcaroladams.net**

Notes

1. Links to publications are available at: http://drcaroladams.net/about-carol/publications/

2. Links to articles in the media are available at: http://drcaroladams.net/about-carol/in-the-media/

3. See http://www.accountingforsustainability.org/

4. All quotes from Paul Druckman in this book are taken from my interview with him at: http://drcaroladams.net/integrated-reporting-what-it-is-and-is-not-an-interview-with-paul-druckman/

5. All references to paragraphs (e.g. para. 1.18) refer to the International <IR> Framework (IIRC, 2013a).

6. Sasol's Annual Integrated Report for 2014 is available at: http://www.sasol.com/investor-centre/publications/integrated-report-1

7. An interview with Damien Walsh on integrated reporting is available at: http://drcaroladams.net/next-steps-in-integrated-thinking-an-interview-with-bankmecus-ceo-damien-walsh/

8. See also 'Linking Stakeholder Engagement and Strategy in Universities' at: http://drcaroladams.net

9. For an analysis of bankmecu's integrated reporting, see http://drcaroladams.net/next-steps-in-integrated-reporting-bankmecu/

10. See http://www.bankmecu.com.au/why-bank-with-us/corporate/customer-value.html

11. All submissions to the Consultation Draft of the International Integrated

Reporting <IR> Framework were posted on the IIRC's website **http://www. theiirc.org/**

12. **http://www.youtube.com/watch?v=-PIZFtZXSa8&list=PLnF8iaZwgjXnpk-FV1PvRH0-DGjrSDSwS&index=7**

13. For further discussion, see **http://drcaroladams.net/integrated-reporting-thinking/**

14. For further discussion on the implications of <IR> for thinking about business models, see **http://drcaroladams.net/understanding-how-sustainability-fits-into-your-business-model/**

15. HSBC reports are available at: **http://www.hsbc.com/investor-relations**

16. For further discussion, see **http://drcaroladams.net/integrated-reporting-and-the-six-capitals-what-does-it-all-mean/**

17. Sasol's Annual Integrated Report for 2014 is available at: **http://www.sasol. com/investor-centre/publications/integrated-report-1**

18. Vodocom's 2012 Integrated Report is available at: **http://vodacom.onlinereport. co.za/vodacom_ir_2012/wp-content/themes/vodacom/downloads/ Vodacom_Integrated_report_2012.pdf**

19. CIMA's 2013 annual report is available at: **http://www.cimaglobal.com/About-us/2013-annual-report/**

20. ACCA's 2013 annual report is available at: **http://annualreport.accaglobal. com/assets/PDF/ACCA-Annual-report-BusinessModel.pdf**

21. Unilever's 2013 annual report is available at: **http://www.unilever.com/ investorrelations/annual_reports/AnnualReportandAccounts2013/**. For more information see **http://drcaroladams.net/towards-integrated-thinking-at-unilever/**

22. The RBS Group's RBS Sustainability Review 2013 is available at: **http://www. rbs.com/content/dam/rbs/Documents/Sustainability/RBS_Sustainability_ Report_2013.pdf**. For a review of this report see **http://drcaroladams.net/rbs-sustainability-review-2013-building-trust-integrated-thinking/**

23. The Fuji Xerox Australia Sustainability Report 2013 is available at: **http://www. fxasustainability.com.au/2013/sustainability-and-strategy/**

24. The IIRC's Emerging Integrated Reporting Database can be accessed at: **http://www.theiirc.org/resources-2/other-publications/emerging-integrated-reporting-database/**

25. Details of award winners can be accessed here: **http://www.corporateregister. com/downloads/files.html**

For Product Safety Concerns and Information please contact our EU
representative GPSR@taylorandfrancis.com
Taylor & Francis Verlag GmbH, Kaufingerstraße 24, 80331 München, Germany

www.ingramcontent.com/pod-product-compliance
Ingram Content Group UK Ltd.
Pitfield, Milton Keynes, MK11 3LW, UK
UKHW040928180425
457613UK00011B/295